TREETOPS

The Three Musketeers

AND THE AFFAIR OF THE QUEEN'S DIAMONDS

WRITTEN BY
ALEXANDRE DUMAS

Adapted by Susan Gates
Illustrated by Daniel Postgate

OXFORD
UNIVERSITY PRESS

OXFORD
UNIVERSITY PRESS

is a department of the University of Oxford.
It furthers the University's objective of excellence in research, scholarship,
and education by publishing worldwide in

Oxford New York

Auckland Cape Town Dar es Salaam Hong Kong Karachi
Kuala Lumpur Madrid Melbourne Mexico City Nairobi
New Delhi Shanghai Taipei Toronto

With offices in

Argentina Austria Brazil Chile Czech Republic France Greece
Guatemala Hungary Italy Japan Poland Portugal Singapore
South Korea Switzerland Thailand Turkey Ukraine Vietnam

Oxford is a registered trade mark of Oxford University Press
in the UK and in certain other countries

Text © Susan Gates 2008

The moral rights of the author have been asserted

Database right Oxford University Press (maker)

First published 2008

All rights reserved. No part of this publication may be reproduced,
stored in a retrieval system, or transmitted, in any form or by any means,
without the prior permission in writing of Oxford University Press,
or as expressly permitted by law, or under terms agreed with the appropriate
reprographics rights organization. Enquiries concerning reproduction
outside the scope of the above should be sent to the Rights Department,
Oxford University Press, at the address above

You must not circulate this book in any other binding or cover
and you must impose this same condition on any acquirer

British Library Cataloguing in Publication Data

Data available

ISBN: 978-0-19-911761-1

10 9 8 7

Cover illustration by Andy Parker

Inside illustrations by Daniel Postgate

Printed in Malaysia by
MunSang Printers Sdn Bhd

Paper used in the production of this book is a natural, recyclable product
made from wood grown in sustainable forests. The manufacturing process
conforms to the environmental regulations of the country of origin.

Contents

Chapter 1:	'You won't escape!'	5
Chapter 2:	'I want to be a musketeer!'	11
Chapter 3:	Three duels	19
Chapter 4:	'Better death than dishonour'	26
Chapter 5:	The queen's secret	35
Chapter 6:	Danger in the palace	45
Chapter 7:	The missing diamonds	54
Chapter 8:	A matter of life or death	60
Chapter 9:	'All for one and one for all!'	69

CHAPTER I

'You won't escape!'

In April 1675, a young man rode into a small town in France. His name was d'Artagnan,* and he was on his way to Paris to seek his fortune and join the king's musketeers.*

D'Artagnan was eighteen years old. He was riding an ancient yellow horse, all skin and bones, called Rosinante. Yet he gazed proudly about him. His blue shirt was old and faded, but his defiant look said, 'I'm as good as you are!' He came from a noble family, even though they were as poor as church mice.

D'Artagnan clopped on Rosinante up to The Jolly Miller Inn. There were three men outside, pointing at him and laughing.

'Are they laughing at *me?*' thought d'Artagnan, his hand clenched tight on his sword hilt. 'How dare they?'

But no, it was Rosinante they were sniggering about!

'Is that a horse I see, or a buttercup?' joked one man. This stranger was tall and handsome, with dark hair and very pale skin. He had a scar on his face. While his friends roared at his joke, he only gave a faint, flickering smile. There was something dangerous and sinister about him.

But d'Artagnan was too angry to notice. His face was flushed with rage. His blood pounded in his ears.

'Sir!' he shouted to the stranger. 'If you insult* my horse, you insult me! And nobody insults me and gets away with it!' He drew his sword and waved it about excitedly.

The stranger stared with cool disbelief at the furious young man. He didn't seem worried at all. 'You really want to fight me?' he asked calmly. 'Are you mad? You don't stand a chance.'

But d'Artagnan drew his sword and rushed forward. He lunged* at the stranger.

The stranger skipped aside. 'I can't waste time killing this young puppy,' he whispered to his friends. 'I'm on a top secret mission for the cardinal.* Deal with him.'

D'Artagnan made another wild lunge. But the stranger had gone. He'd slipped away.

D'Artagnan stared frantically around. 'Where are you, you coward?' he cried. 'You won't escape from me!'

But then he staggered under a hail of blows. The man's friends were attacking him.

D'Artagnan fought back bravely.

'Give in, you stubborn idiot!' yelled one man.

'Never!' shrieked d'Artagnan, crumpling to his knees.

But then the inn's servants joined in. One of them felled d'Artagnan with a floor mop and knocked him out cold.

When d'Artagnan woke up in the bedroom of the inn, his head was wrapped in bandages. At first he just felt sick and dizzy. He felt his throbbing head, and groaned. Then he remembered that he'd been insulted. On wobbly legs, he stumbled downstairs.

'Where is that man with the scar?' D'Artagnan demanded.

'Sir,' said the innkeeper, 'please sit down before you fall down.'

D'Artagnan collapsed into a chair. In a faint but <u>ferocious</u> voice, he said, 'I have a fight to finish! I must defend my honour!'

'Sir,' said the innkeeper soothingly, 'you are a brave young man, and we all admire you for it. But I should forget about that stranger. He's a dangerous fellow. He has powerful friends. And, besides, you couldn't fight a flea at the moment.'

D'Artagnan was a <u>hot-headed</u> young man. But he was no fool. He could see the sense of the innkeeper's advice.

But he wasn't going to forget about the stranger with the scarred face. He felt sure that they were destined to meet again. 'And then I'll have my revenge,' he muttered to himself.

Outside the inn, his old horse, Rosinante, was peacefully eating the grass. D'Artagnan scrambled onto her skinny back.

'To Paris, Rosinante!' cried d'Artagnan, as the yellow nag plodded off. 'I have an appointment with Monsieur de Treville,* the captain of the king's musketeers!'

CHAPTER 2

'I want to be a musketeer!'

D'Artagnan was almost late for his meeting with Monsieur de Treville. There was a crowd of king's musketeers outside the captain's house. They were a wild, unruly bunch. They swaggered about, shouting and arguing and clanking their swords.

But to d'Artagnan they were all heroes, supermen. It was the dream of his life to be a musketeer like them.

They took no notice of the shabby young man trying to find his way through the mob.

When d'Artagnan reached Monsieur de Treville's office, no one took any notice of him

there either. Monsieur de Treville had two musketeers lined up in front of his desk. And he was giving them a good telling-off.

'Porthos, Aramis,' he told them. 'I hear you and Athos have been quarrelling again with the cardinal's men.'

Next to the king, the cardinal was the most powerful man in France. Some said he *was* the most powerful. For the king was a weak man. And the cardinal was cunning and clever. He could make the king do anything he wanted.

'But Monsieur de Treville,' boomed one musketeer in a loud, ringing voice. 'The cardinal's men insulted the queen! So we were forced to defend her honour!'

The cardinal was the queen's deadly enemy. His spies watched her constantly. He was always plotting to turn the king against her.

'Hmm,' said Monsieur de Treville dryly. 'Are you sure that wasn't just an excuse for a fight?'

Porthos swirled his crimson cloak around. He was a giant of a man, as burly and strong as a bear. 'But sir!' he bellowed. 'They were making rude jokes about the queen and Lord Buckingham.'*

Everyone in Paris knew that the English lord was madly in love with the queen. But did the queen return his love? The cardinal was desperate to prove she did. For that would certainly lead to the queen's downfall, or even her execution.*

'Besides,' added Aramis. 'It was only a *little* fight. Just a scuffle.'

Porthos was swaggering and loud, and dressed like a peacock. But his friend Aramis was the exact opposite. He was modest and quietly spoken. His clothes weren't showy at all, but neat and sombre.

'Scuffle?' said Monsieur de Treville. 'I hear you two and Athos wounded thirteen of the cardinal's men!'

'Rubbish!' bragged Porthos, rattling his great sword. 'We felled at least twenty of them. Anyway, they started it.'

'Tut, tut,' said Monsieur de Treville. 'You

have the courage of lions. But sometimes you musketeers behave like children. Where's Athos? He's the most sensible of the three of you!'

Aramis started to say, 'He was wounded, sir, in the shoulder...' when the door opened and a tall, handsome musketeer came in.

'You sent for me, sir?' he asked, in a calm voice. He swayed slightly. His face was very pale. It was clear his wound was hurting him.

'My dear Athos!' said Monsieur de Treville, all his sternness disappearing. 'You shouldn't be here! Take him back to his house, you two. Put him to bed.'

'At once, sir,' cried Porthos, saluting smartly, pleased to be let off the hook. And he and Aramis helped their friend Athos out of Monsieur de Treville's office.

'And keep out of trouble,' Monsieur de Treville warned.

All this time, d'Artagnan had been standing unnoticed in the shadows. Then Monsieur de Treville began signing papers and still didn't see him. D'Artagnan gave an embarrassed cough. Monsieur de Treville looked up in surprise and saw a tall, lanky young man shuffling about awkwardly in front of his desk.

'Who are you?' he asked.

'I'm d'Artagnan, sir. I had an appointment to see you.'

At first Monsieur de Treville looked blank. Then he said, 'I know! Your father was a good friend of mine. And a brave and loyal soldier.

Now what can I do for his son?'

'I want to be a musketeer,' said d'Artagnan eagerly. 'I want to defend our king and queen. Like those fine men I just saw in your office.'

Monsieur de Treville's answer was kind but firm. 'Each of those fine men you saw has proved himself by many brave and heroic deeds. Only then can a man join the king's musketeers.'

D'Artagnan controlled his disappointment well. 'I understand, sir,' he nodded. 'It's a great honour to be in the musketeers. Naturally I have to earn my place. I'll try my very best to prove myself worthy.'

Monsieur de Treville was just thinking, 'What a wise and mature young man,' when suddenly d'Artagnan happened to glance out of the window.

A man was passing in the street outside. He was wrapped in a black cloak, with a hood. But d'Artagnan had sharp eyes. And he could clearly see, under the hood, pale skin, dark hair and a scarred cheek.

'It's him!' he cried.

'Who?' asked a confused Monsieur de Treville.

'The mysterious stranger from The Jolly Miller Inn,' cried d'Artagnan. 'The one who insulted my horse, Rosinante, then refused to fight with me! The cowardly rat! Well, he won't escape me this time!'

D'Artagnan drew his sword and dashed excitedly out of the door.

Monsieur de Treville stared after him. He shook his head. 'And I thought he was sensible. But he's a reckless, sword-waving hothead.' Then Monsieur de Treville grinned to himself as he bent over his papers again. 'Mind you, that means he'll probably make a very good musketeer.'

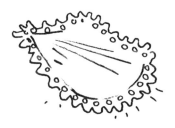

CHAPTER 3

Three duels

D'Artagnan raced out of Monsieur de Treville's office and down the stairs.

The stranger with the scarred face had been walking slowly along the street outside. If d'Artagnan hurried, he could easily catch up with him.

D'Artagnan took the steps three at a time, head down like a charging bull. Suddenly, he ran into someone.

'Please get out of my way,' panted d'Artagnan.

But instead of moving, the person he'd head-butted grabbed him. D'Artagnan looked up. It was Athos, who should have been in bed, but wasn't. His face looked sickly grey. In his mad rush to catch the stranger, d'Artagnan had run into the musketeer's wounded shoulder.

'I do apologise,' gabbled d'Artagnan. 'But I'm in a great hurry.'

Athos let him go. He was the most commanding and dignified of the three musketeers. He glared angrily at the young man.

'Your manners are bad, sir,' he told d'Artagnan. 'You behave like a country bumpkin.'

D'Artagnan had been racing off again. But at these words, he turned back, his face flushed with fury.

'You insult me, sir!' he cried. 'I may be from the country. But I'm no bumpkin! Unfortunately, I can't fight you now. But name the time and the place…'*

'Midday today,' said Athos promptly. 'Outside the convent.'*

'Fine,' said d'Artagnan as he dashed away. 'I'll be there.'

He ran faster than ever, dodging through the crowd of musketeers. Whatever happened, he mustn't let the mysterious stranger escape him again.

Suddenly, d'Artagnan was wrapped up in crimson velvet. He tried to fight his way free.

'Hey!' yelled a booming voice. 'Mind my cloak. That cost fifty crowns!'*

D'Artagnan managed to untangle himself.

He found himself staring into the furious face of Porthos, who was very vain about his gorgeous clothes.

'Sorry, sorry,' said d'Artagnan. 'But I have to catch someone...'

'Clumsy young idiot!' thundered Porthos, inspecting his cloak. 'If you've torn it, I'll give you a good thrashing!'

'Oh, will you?' said d'Artagnan in a sudden fury. 'Not if I can help it!'

'Then let's settle this matter!' roared Porthos, as d'Artagnan raced away. 'One o'clock at the convent!'

'I look forward to it!' D'Artagnan flung back defiantly over his shoulder.

At last d'Artagnan was out of the crowd. But there was no sign of the stranger. D'Artagnan raced up and down the street, peering into doorways and down alleys.

Finally he sank to his knees, exhausted. 'It's no good, I've lost him,' he gasped.

Now the frantic chase was over, d'Artagnan began to calm down. His good sense returned.

'You've made a mess of things today,' he scolded himself.

Not only had he upset Monsieur de Treville, by dashing rudely out of his office. But he was due to fight two duels,* each with a musketeer who could kill ten d'Artagnans if he chose.

D'Artagnan shook his head despairingly. 'You've been a silly idiot,' he told himself sorrowfully. But then his confidence bounced back. He'd just spotted the third musketeer, Aramis, in the street. He was the slender, well-groomed, quiet one with the boyish face. Aramis was talking to two friends.

'I shall be very friendly and polite to him,' d'Artagnan decided, 'to make up for my rude behaviour to Athos and Porthos.'

And he saw the perfect chance. Aramis had dropped a handkerchief out of his pocket. He seemed to be trying to hide it under his foot.

But that didn't stop d'Artagnan. He raced up and yanked the hankie from under Aramis's boot. It was a beautiful, embroidered hankie, probably a noble lady's.

D'Artagnan presented it to Aramis with a low bow. 'You dropped this, I believe.'

Immediately, Aramis blushed scarlet. He snatched the handkerchief from d'Artagnan's hand. 'What business is this of yours, sir?'

'Oh no,' thought d'Artagnan. 'Have I done the wrong thing again?'

It seems he had, for Aramis's friends hooted with glee. 'Aramis, you sly devil,' said one. 'You pretend to be so shy of ladies. Yet here you are, carrying around a present from one of them in your pockets!' They went off, still laughing loudly.

Aramis scowled at d'Artagnan. 'Sir,' he said, 'now the whole world knows my secrets, thanks to you! You clumsy oaf!'

Again d'Artagnan felt his temper rising. He struggled to control himself. But it was no good. His pride was too deeply hurt.

'Sir!' he burst out. 'No one calls me a clumsy oaf and gets away with it! Take out your sword.'

But then he remembered it was nearly twelve o'clock and he had two duels to fight before settling this argument.

'Is two o'clock all right?' he asked Aramis.

'Perfect,' said Aramis. 'For I have to act as second* at twelve to a friend who is also fighting a duel.'

'At the convent then!' cried d'Artagnan, as he raced away.

'Wait a minute,' said Aramis. 'That's where I'm going now.'

But d'Artagnan was already too far away to hear.

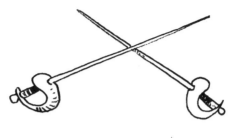

CHAPTER 4

'Better death than dishonour'*

D'Artagnan hurried to the convent for his duel with Athos. His thoughts were serious now. D'Artagnan was no fool and he knew one or other of the musketeers would kill him. They were experienced soldiers who'd proved themselves in many wars. And d'Artagnan, although he was skilled with a sword, had never fought a duel in his life.

'Courage!' he urged himself. He was sure this would be his last day on earth. But still he wasn't going to run like a coward. 'Better death than dishonour,' d'Artagnan told himself.

But there was a chill down his spine and his stomach was churning. The convent was a grim, forbidding ruin. Beside it was a little piece of waste ground. Although duelling was against the law, gentlemen often met here to fight, in secret.

Athos was waiting, looking cool and unconcerned, even though his wound still hurt him badly.

'Sorry I'm late,' gasped d'Artagnan.

'That's quite all right,' said Athos graciously. 'I'm still waiting for my two friends. They're acting as my seconds.'

'Oh dear,' thought d'Artagnan. He'd clean forgotten about seconds – friends who came to watch a duel, to make sure the fight was fair.

'I'm afraid I have no seconds,' he told Athos politely. 'I only arrived today in Paris and I don't know a soul! I do apologise.'

Athos was just as polite back. 'I apologise as well,' he said bowing low. 'My seconds are late. Where are those rogues? They should be here!'

At that moment, a familiar voice roared, 'Hey, Athos, sorry we're late!' The giant figure of Porthos appeared. He strode up, his crimson cloak swirling.

Behind him strolled the slender Aramis, soberly dressed and discreet as always. He hid his thoughts, while everything Porthos felt could be instantly seen on his face.

'Have you killed him yet?' roared Porthos eagerly. 'Who was the foolish fellow anyway?'

'I'm the foolish fellow,' said d'Artagnan, stepping forward and bowing. 'And we haven't started yet. We were waiting for you.'

Porthos goggled at him in astonishment. 'Wait a minute! Aren't I fighting you here at one o'clock?'

'And I at two,' added Aramis, in his soft voice.

'Well, young man,' said Athos, 'it seems you have a busy couple of hours ahead.'

'Let's get on with it then,' cried d'Artagnan, drawing his sword. 'On guard!'*

And he was about to cross swords* with Athos, when a band of armed men came riding around the corner.

'The cardinal's men!'* frowned Athos.

They were the deadly enemies of the king's musketeers. And now the cardinal's men had caught them, red-handed,* breaking the law. They could be put in prison, even executed, for duelling.

'Put your swords away, gentlemen!' shouted Jussac, who led the cardinal's men. 'And prepare to be arrested!'

'We mustn't get taken to prison!' hissed Porthos. 'Monsieur de Treville would be furious. Remember his orders this morning – "Keep out of trouble."'

'I'm afraid, gentlemen,' said Athos calmly to the cardinal's men, 'we can't allow you to arrest us.'

'Don't be foolish,' said Jussac. 'You're not thinking of fighting, are you? There are six of us. And only three of you.'

'Four!' cried d'Artagnan, leaping to the side of the three musketeers.

'Do you know what you're doing?' said Jussac. 'Get out of our way, young man.'

'He's right,' whispered Athos. 'This isn't

your fight. Go now, while you still can. This is no place for a boy.'

But d'Artagnan had made his choice. 'It's Athos, Porthos, Aramis and d'Artagnan!' he cried, charging at the cardinal's men.

The three musketeers rushed in to back him up. But d'Artagnan found himself face to face with the great Jussac himself, a famous swordsman and veteran* of many battles.

Jussac had more skill, but d'Artagnan had speed and youth on his side. Jussac had a struggle to hold him off.

'This is ridiculous,' Jussac thought as he thrust and parried with his rapier.* 'How can a boy like this be such hard work?'

Suddenly, d'Artagnan made a lunge and wounded Jussac in the arm. The cardinal's man dropped his sword. Instantly, d'Artagnan rushed off to fight someone else.

'Hmm,' thought Athos, who was coolly fighting left-handed.* 'That young man has spirit! I'm glad I didn't have to kill him.'

The fighting raged for several more minutes,

Porthos joking all the time with his opponent. 'Ha ha! Missed me *again!*'

Then Jussac shouted, 'Stop fighting!' Four of the cardinal's men were wounded and this was a battle they couldn't win. 'Withdraw!'* he said bitterly. And to the king's musketeers he said, 'We'll get you next time!'

'What a victory!' bragged Porthos, as the cardinal's men staggered back to their horses and galloped off. 'Wait until we tell everyone!'

'Best keep quiet,' advised Aramis. 'We don't want Monsieur de Treville hearing about it. We'll have a private celebration, just for ourselves.' And the three musketeers linked arms and strode down the street.

D'Artagnan was hanging back. No one had invited him to the party. Why should they? He wasn't even a musketeer. But he knew he'd fought well and he couldn't help his face crumbling in disappointment.

But then Aramis called to him, 'Come and join us.'

'Yes!' roared Porthos. 'You wounded the

great Jussac. He'll never live it down! Beaten by a country boy!'

This time, d'Artagnan wasn't insulted. For Athos added quietly, 'Well done. You fought bravely,' and linked arms with him.

All four of them strode out together, laughing and joking, and taking up the whole street. Porthos had a blue hat, as big as a cartwheel, with a great curling feather in it. He spun it into the air and caught it again.

'All for one and one for all!'* he cheered.

'All for one and one for all!' cried the others. And d'Artagnan roared the loudest of them all.

CHAPTER 5

The queen's secret

After d'Artagnan had fought so bravely on their side, Athos, Porthos and Aramis took him under their wing. D'Artagnan went everywhere with them. The four of them became a familiar sight in Paris, striding through the streets, laughing and joking.

D'Artagnan was glad to be their friend. But he wasn't satisfied. 'When will my big chance come?' he fretted. He wanted to do something bold and daring. Something that would persuade Monsieur de Treville to make him a musketeer. He was even more determined now to become one of them. The day he put on the uniform of the king's musketeers would be the proudest of his life.

One day, d'Artagnan was sitting alone in his lodgings. He was wondering, as always, how to impress Monsieur de Treville. But he had another problem too. He was flat broke.* He hadn't paid his rent for three months. He didn't even have enough money to buy himself a loaf of bread. And, as we know, d'Artagnan was far too proud to tell anyone how poor he was.

Suddenly, his door crashed open. It was his landlord, Monsieur Bonacieux, who lived downstairs.

'If it's about the rent…' d'Artagnan began to say.

'No, no, it's not about that,' cried Monsieur Bonacieux. He was a quiet little man, who usually d'Artagnan hardly noticed. But today he was frantic and wild-eyed. 'You must help me!' he begged d'Artagnan. 'My wife has been kidnapped!'

'Kidnapped?' echoed d'Artagnan, shocked. 'How do you know?'

'The neighbours saw her being bundled into a carriage. By a man with a scar on his cheek…'

'Was he tall and dark?' asked d'Artagnan excitedly. 'With pale skin?'

'Yes!' said Monsieur Bonacieux amazed. 'How did you know that?'

'Because I've met him before,' said d'Artagnan. 'He's the stranger from The Jolly Miller Inn!'

'Well, he's no stranger to me,' said Monsieur Bonacieux. 'My wife pointed him out in the street, just the other day. She said, "Beware of that man. He is Rochefort, the cardinal's chief spy."'

'Good heavens,' said d'Artagnan, amazed. 'So that's who he is! I thought there was something sinister about him. But why would the cardinal want him to kidnap your wife?'

'Because my wife is the queen's maid. She's more than a maid – she's a loyal friend. She knows all the queen's secrets. And there's one secret the cardinal is desperate to discover.'

D'Artagnan nodded wisely, as if he knew all about the politics at court.

'It's about Lord Buckingham, of course,' the little landlord rushed on. 'We all know he's madly in love with the queen. And some say he's in Paris at the moment, trying to see her. The cardinal wants to know if that's true or not. And whether Buckingham and the queen plan to meet secretly. That's why he's kidnapped my wife. To make her tell him. Oh dear, oh dear,' said the landlord wringing his hands. 'I'll never see her again!'

D'Artagnan was really interested now.

He sensed adventure. The fact that it had a royal link made it even more thrilling. For musketeers were sworn to protect the queen at all times.

He was even more interested when Bonacieux said, 'If you find my wife, I'll let you off the rent you owe. And give you a big reward besides.'

'The money isn't important,' lied d'Artagnan haughtily. 'But I have a score to settle with that Rochefort fellow.'

'So you'll help me?' cried the little landlord. 'Oh thank you, thank you!'

Monsieur Bonacieux leaped up and dashed to the door. 'I'm going to scour the streets of Paris* for that carriage.'

The hot-headed d'Artagnan was going to dash out too, to search for the missing Madame* Bonacieux and her kidnapper, Rochefort. But for once, his good sense stopped him. 'The cardinal will have hidden her away by now,' he told himself. 'But where?'

Then he had a brainwave. 'I'll ask Porthos, Aramis and Athos!' They knew much more about the cardinal's scheming than he did. Perhaps they could suggest where poor Madame Bonacieux might be.

D'Artagnan sprang up, eager to rescue a lady in danger. It has to be said, he would have been even more eager if Madame Bonacieux had been young and pretty. He'd never actually seen her. But since his landlord was a dull and doddery person, d'Artagnan guessed his wife would be too.

'But musketeers must be gallant* to all ladies!' d'Artagnan told himself.

Suddenly, he heard a commotion in the room below him. Men were shouting, 'Do as you're told! The cardinal wants to see you!' There were shrill shrieks of 'Let me go, you brutes! Help! Help!'

D'Artagnan didn't hesitate. He went rushing downstairs and kicked in the door. A young woman was struggling with three men, who were trying to tie her hands.

'Leave that lady alone!' roared d'Artagnan, outraged.

Two of the men took one look at the furious, sword waving d'Artagnan and dived out of the window. D'Artagnan clashed swords with the third. But after a few minutes of lunging and slashing, the man lost heart and ran out of the door.

The lady sank fainting into a chair.

'Are you all right?' asked d'Artagnan anxiously. He had time now to see that she was very pretty.

The lady opened her eyes, 'Thank you, sir,' she said. 'You have saved me. I am Madame Bonacieux.'

'Madame Bonacieux!' cried d'Artagnan amazed. 'But I thought you'd been kidnapped!'

'I had,' said Madame Bonacieux.

D'Artagnan noticed she had eyes of the deepest blue.

'But I escaped,' she continued, 'by climbing down knotted sheets from a window.' Then she said, more warily, 'Did my husband tell you who kidnapped me, and why?'

'He did,' said d'Artagnan. 'He told me the whole story. But don't fear, madame. I, too, am a friend of the queen. I'll do anything I can to be of service to you or her.'

But Madame Bonacieux had recovered from her fright. She got up briskly and put on a blue cloak that matched her eyes. D'Artagnan watched her with dismay and asked, 'Where are you going?'

'Once again, I thank you for rescuing me,' said Madame Bonacieux. 'But I have important business to attend to.'

'Let me come with you!' cried d'Artagnan. 'What if the cardinal's men try to kidnap you again?'

'Don't worry about me,' said Madame Bonacieux. 'I can look after myself.' She put up the hood of her cloak. 'Don't follow me,' she ordered him. Then she slipped out of the door and was gone.

D'Artagnan stared after her. He forgot how

clever and brave she must be. She had clearly been carrying out dangerous missions for the queen, and she had just escaped from Rochefort, the cardinal's best spy.

'She needs my help!' d'Artagnan decided. 'I'll follow her, without her knowing.'

He hurried upstairs to his lodgings. He too wrapped himself in a long cloak, with the hood up. Then he slipped out of the door after Madame Bonacieux.

CHAPTER 6

Danger in the palace

D'Artagnan flitted through Paris after Madame Bonacieux. It was getting dark now and he often lost sight of her in the twisting, turning streets. But then he would glimpse her blue cloak in the distance, and rush to catch up.

All the time he was trailing her, d'Artagnan's head was spinning. He'd only known her for twenty minutes. But those beautiful blue eyes had bewitched him. He had fallen head over heels in love with Madame Bonacieux.

'Of course, I can't tell her,' d'Artagnan told himself, 'because she's a married lady. But in any case my love is noble and pure! All I want is to protect her. I'd die for her if I had to!'

Carried away by his romantic dream, he turned a corner. And there was his beloved Madame Bonacieux, in a pool of moonlight. A man slid out of the shadows and crept towards her. He too was hidden in a long cloak. A large hat hid his face.

'He's a thief!' thought d'Artagnan frantically. 'He's going to rob her!'

He drew his sword and rushed forward. 'You villain, sir!' cried d'Artagnan. 'Leave that lady alone! She is under my protection!'

The stranger instantly drew his own sword. Blades flashed in the moonlight.

Then Madame Bonacieux recognised d'Artagnan. 'I told you not to follow me!' she cried. 'This man means me no harm.' Her voice sank to a whisper. 'It's the Duke of Buckingham. I'm taking him to a secret meeting with the queen.'

'Oh no!' thought d'Artagnan, realising he'd made a dreadful mistake. 'Your pardon, sir,' he said, bowing deeply to the English noble.

The duke didn't look at all flustered. He was rich, powerful and supremely arrogant. He smiled coolly at his fiery young challenger. 'A man after my own heart,' he said, in perfect French.

Madame Bonacieux wasn't as calm as the duke. 'Now, go,' she hissed to d'Artagnan, her eyes flickering around the street. 'The cardinal has spies everywhere!'

This secret meeting between the queen and the duke was desperately risky. But the duke wasn't at all nervous. His eyes gleamed at the thought of the danger ahead.

'Let this young man come with us,' he told Madame Bonacieux. 'He has spirit. I like that! And we shall need a guard.'

So d'Artagnan found himself following the famous English duke and Madame Bonacieux, the queen's maid, to the Louvre,* the royal palace where the queen of France lived.

Madame Bonacieux had planned all this. She knew every nook and cranny of the palace.

She led them through a side door, which she unlocked, and across courtyards, down corridors, and up dark, twisty staircases.

At last she opened a secret door, hidden in the wooden panelling.

'Stay outside!' whispered Madame Bonacieux. 'Warn us if anyone comes.'

She took the duke with her into the room.

D'Artagnan did as he was told and stayed outside, his sword drawn, every nerve alert for danger.

After about fifteen minutes, Madame Bonacieux came out with the duke. D'Artagnan saw that the duke clutched a little rosewood box, as if it was the most precious thing in the world.

'I wonder if the queen gave him that?' thought d'Artagnan.

But no one told him anything. Swiftly, Madame Bonacieux led them back the way they had come and out of the palace. The queen, meanwhile, hurried back to the safety of her bedroom.

Back in the secret room where the duke and queen had just met, a sneeze came from behind a wall tapestry.* A lady-in-waiting* slid out. She sneezed again, 'Atishoo!' and shook the spiders' webs and dust out of her hair.

She was another of the cardinal's spies. She'd followed the queen to the secret room and hidden behind the tapestry. She'd heard every word the duke and queen said to each other.

She opened the door of the room and looked cautiously up and down the corridor. 'All clear,' she thought. Then she rushed off to report to her master, the cardinal.

Half an hour later, in the cardinal's house, she was telling him and Rochefort her story.

The cardinal was a man to be feared. He was fiercely intelligent, a brilliant soldier and a ruthless politician.* He could easily twist the king around his little finger. The queen was harder to deal with – she wasn't as weak as her husband. So the cardinal wanted to ruin her, have her put to death if possible, and replace her with a queen he could control.

He fixed the lady-in-waiting with his piercing gaze. 'So you didn't hear the queen say that she loved the duke?'

'N-no, your eminence,'* stuttered the woman. 'In fact, she said she *didn't*. She said she was only meeting him to tell him that. She said they must never meet again. That it was far too dangerous.'

'Hmm.' The cardinal stroked his small grey beard. He shot a glance at his chief spy, Rochefort. That wasn't what they wanted to hear.

'Then Lord Buckingham asked for a token,'* said the lady-in-waiting nervously. 'Something to remember her by.'

'A token?' said Rochefort keenly. 'So did the queen give it? Quick, tell us!'

He strode towards the spy, as if he wanted to shake the information out of her.

'Yes, sir,' she answered hastily. 'She had to. The duke swore that if she didn't, he'd never leave France. So the queen gave him a little

51

rosewood box. In it were two diamonds from the necklace his majesty the king gave her on her birthday.'

The cardinal and his chief spy glanced again at each other. But this time there was triumph in their eyes.

'That is all,' snapped the cardinal, dismissing the lady-in-waiting.

When she'd scurried away, the cardinal gloated, 'This is the chance we've been waiting for!'

His quick brain was already plotting the queen's downfall. 'I'll get the king to arrange a ball for the queen,' he told Rochefort. 'And to insist she wears her diamond necklace. When the king sees two of the diamonds are missing, I'll tell him why. I'll make him believe, of course, that the queen has betrayed him and is madly in love with the duke.'

The cardinal smiled a sinister smile. 'I think, at last, we have her majesty in our grasp.'

Then he became brisk and businesslike. He gave Rochefort his orders. 'When the queen knows about the ball, she'll panic. I predict she'll send messengers to England to get back the diamonds. You must find those messengers. And you must stop them, at all costs, from reaching Buckingham.'

'Leave it to me,' said Rochefort, his voice grim. 'Her messengers will never leave France alive.'

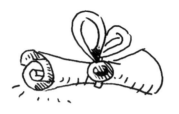

CHAPTER 7

The missing diamonds

The next evening, d'Artagnan was sitting in his lodgings with Athos, Porthos and Aramis. He was telling them about the secret meeting in the palace of the Louvre.

'Are you saying,' boomed Porthos, crashing his fist on the table, 'that the queen of France was as close to you as I am now?'

'Actually, there was a wall between us,' admitted d'Artagnan.

Athos, who was always wise and cool-headed, frowned. 'Watch your back,' he warned d'Artagnan. 'If the cardinal finds out you were involved, he'll have you arrested.'

At that moment there was a frantic knocking on d'Artagnan's door. D'Artagnan opened it a crack. Behind him, the three musketeers had already drawn their swords.

D'Artagnan peered out. Two eyes, of the deepest blue, peered back. 'Madame Bonacieux!' he cried. He threw the door wide open, his heart pounding.

'I've come to ask you a great favour,' she began.

'I'll do anything for you!' cried d'Artagnan rashly.

'It's the queen who needs your help,' said Madame Bonacieux. 'I wouldn't ask since you're hardly a man yet. But the queen is desperate.'

'Oh,' said d'Artagnan, crushed to find that his beloved thought him little more than a child.

'You'd better come in,' he said, crestfallen. But Madame Bonacieux shrank back when she saw three armed men inside.

'It's all right,' d'Artagnan assured her.

'These men are my friends. They are king's musketeers, sworn to defend the queen to the death.'

'King's musketeers?' said Madame Bonacieux. She came hesitantly into the room. Her gaze swept over them. Could they be trusted? She decided she had no choice.

'Gentlemen,' she said. 'Your queen is in deadly danger.'

She told them all about the diamond necklace. How, in four days from now, the queen had to wear it at the ball. How the queen was sure this was the cardinal's wicked scheme.

'He'll use the missing diamonds to ruin her,' said Madame Bonacieux. 'He may even demand her death.'

'So her majesty must get them back,' said Aramis, in his quiet voice, 'in time for the ball.'

'That's right,' said Madame Bonacieux. 'But Buckingham is already back in London. So someone must ride like the wind to get the diamonds. It will be very dangerous. The queen's enemies are everywhere.'

'I'll go!' cried d'Artagnan, suddenly cheering up. After all, an adventure like this would really impress Monsieur de Treville. 'He's bound to make me a musketeer,' thought d'Artagnan. '*If* I come back alive.'

Then a calm voice interrupted his dreams of glory. 'We'll all go,' said Athos. 'Our young friend will need some help.'

'I agree!' roared Porthos. 'All for one and one for all!'

'Then you must start now,' said Madame Bonacieux. She pulled a letter from her cloak. 'Here's the queen's letter to Buckingham. It has her personal seal.* It asks him to give her messenger the two diamonds.'

'I'll take it.' D'Artagnan stuffed the queen's letter inside his doublet.*

The four sprang into action and clattered down the stairs to get ready for their journey.

Madame Bonacieux slid out after them, put up the hood to her cloak and vanished like a ghost down a dark alleyway.

Across the street, hidden in a doorway, one of the cardinal's spies saw them all leave. He'd been watching Madame Bonacieux's house for some time.

'Those musketeers are the queen's messengers,' he thought. 'I'm sure of it.' And he rushed off to tell Rochefort.

At two o'clock in the morning, d'Artagnan

and the three musketeers left Paris. They were a splendid sight, on fine black horses and armed to the teeth. They rode through the night like shadows, swift and silent. They were heading for Calais, where they would catch a boat to England.

What they didn't know, was that Rochefort had already made plans to stop them.

CHAPTER 8

A matter of life or death

The trouble began at dawn, when the four dust-covered and weary riders stopped briefly to snatch a meal at an inn.

'Don't unsaddle the horses!' called Athos as they hurried inside.

Another traveller turned up as they were having breakfast. He sat watching them quietly.

As they left the stranger stood up. He picked out Porthos, the loudest and most swaggering and said, 'Good health to the cardinal!'

Instantly, Porthos's face flushed with temper. 'I only drink to the king!'

'Then you are a fool!' cried the stranger, drawing his sword.

Porthos drew his, crying, 'You insult me, sir!'

'Calm down,' hissed Aramis. 'This man is deliberately picking a fight!'

But nothing could stop Porthos when his blood was up.* Besides, his honour was at stake.

Athos sighed, as Porthos and the stranger fought all around the kitchen and out into the garden.

'Just polish him off quickly!' yelled Athos. 'And catch us up!'

So now the queen's messengers were down to three. They galloped on. Three miles further the road narrowed. Eight workmen were digging it up with picks and shovels. The riders had to slow down their horses to get past. Suddenly, the workmen threw down their tools and made a dive for their muskets, hidden in the grass.

'It's an ambush!'* cried Athos, as the first shots rang out.

The three riders spurred on their horses but, before they escaped, Aramis got a bullet through his shoulder. Bleeding, he clung onto his horse but by the next town he was too weak to ride.

'Leave me here,' he told the others. 'I'll only slow you down.'

So now the queen's messengers were down to two. 'We'll ride across country,' said Athos. That way, they might avoid Rochefort's traps.

It was getting dark. The horses foamed at the mouth, ridden half to death. Their riders were almost falling off with exhaustion.

'We must water and feed the horses,' said Athos. 'And get some sleep.'

They stopped at a tiny country inn. But the cardinal had spies in the remotest places. And, by sheer bad luck, the landlord of this inn was one of them.

At first, the inn seemed safe. D'Artagnan and Athos put their horses in the stables and managed to grab a few hours sleep. As dawn broke, they got up to ride onwards to Calais.

While d'Artagnan went out to fetch the horses, Athos paid their bill. As he handed over the money, the landlord took two pistols from his desk drawer.

'Put your hands up!' the landlord ordered.

Then four more armed men burst into the room.

Before they seized him, Athos managed to yell, at the top of his voice. 'They've got me, d'Artagnan. Ride for your life!'

Outside, with the horses, d'Artagnan heard his friend's cry. He hated to leave Athos like this. But the musketeer could look after himself. The queen was helpless, surrounded by spies and traitors.*

D'Artagnan sprang onto his horse and galloped away.

So now there was only one queen's messenger.

D'Artagnan reached Calais without any more trouble. But at the town gates, his exhausted horse could not go another step. He had to leave it to recover. He hurried on foot to the harbour, taking a short cut along the beach.

Suddenly a man leaped from the grassy dunes with his sword drawn. D'Artagnan glimpsed dark hair, pale skin, that scar...

'Rochefort,' he breathed as he drew his rapier.

Ever since they'd first met at The Jolly Miller, d'Artagnan had vowed to cross swords with this man. But now was the worst possible time. Once the tide turned* he couldn't catch a boat to England until tomorrow. Then he'd be too late to return the diamonds in time for the ball.

Rochefort was one of the best swordsmen in France. His smile was cool and confident. He was thinking, 'It won't take me long to kill this troublesome boy.'

But d'Artagnan had learned a thing or two since he'd been friends with the three musketeers.

Rochefort skipped back, as d'Artagnan launched a furious attack, his blade flashing in the air.

Rochefort hadn't expected such skill. He parried, lunged. But d'Artagnan slipped in under his guard and with one thrust ran him through.* Rochefort collapsed in the dunes, holding his side. But d'Artagnan didn't feel the satisfaction he'd expected. He was too worried about getting those diamonds. He hurried away, to get the ship to England.

The Duke of Buckingham was dining in his London house when a servant entered the room.

'My lord!' he said. 'There's a young Frenchman downstairs. He's jabbering away, waving his arms about. Very excitable, if you ask me. But it seems he's brought you this letter.'

The duke took the letter. He was going to put it aside to read later. Then he saw the seal. Feverishly he tore it open, and scanned the queen's note. He sprang out of his seat. 'Show the young man up,' he ordered his servant. 'Instantly!'

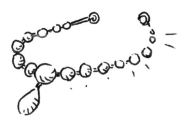

CHAPTER 9

'All for one and one for all!'

'So then what happened?' roared Porthos.

D'Artagnan and the three musketeers were back together again. It was the night after the ball. They were sitting in their favourite inn, having a celebration meal.

'But first I want to hear how you three made it safely back to Paris,' insisted d'Artagnan.

'There was nothing to it really,' said the modest Aramis. 'I had my wound bandaged and rode back.'

'And I managed to get free from my captors,'* said Athos, typically not giving any details of his heroic escape.

'And I fought like a lion!' bragged Porthos, twirling his moustache. 'I fought like ten lions! And finally made the fellow surrender!'

'Now tell us the rest of *your* story,' said the soft-spoken Aramis. 'You'd got to the bit where you picked up the queen's diamonds in London.'

'Oh yes,' said d'Artagnan. 'Well, the duke arranged for a private boat and fresh horses once I reached France. These rich and powerful men can do anything! Anyway, I galloped all night and the next day, and tore into Paris with only an hour to spare before the ball.'

'Yet you look fresh as a daisy today,' said Athos. 'You young men are made of iron.'

'Madame Bonacieux must have given up hope!' boomed Porthos.

'She had,' said d'Artagnan. 'When she saw me outside the Louvre, she cried, "Thank heavens!" for the queen was about to leave for the ball. I got the diamonds back in the nick of time!'

'They say that when the cardinal saw the queen's necklace complete he gnashed his teeth with fury,' laughed Porthos.

'No doubt he'll find other ways to plot against her,' said Aramis gravely.

'Then we musketeers will stop him!' crowed Porthos.

'Except I'm not a musketeer,' said d'Artagnan sadly.

Porthos slapped him on the back. 'Don't look so gloomy, young man. When Monsieur de Treville hears about your amazing courage, he'll make you one of us straight away.'

'That'll be the happiest moment of my life!' said d'Artagnan, his eyes shining.

'All for one and one for all!'

Alexandre Dumas
(born 1802, died 1870)

Alexandre Dumas is one of the most widely read French writers in the world. He was born in a village near Paris. His grandmother was Afro-Caribbean and had been a slave on a French Caribbean island. His grandfather was a French nobleman. Dumas's father was a general in the French army, but he died when Alexandre was only four years old, leaving his family very poor. Dumas's mother told him endless stories of his father's wartime experiences. These gave Dumas a great love of romantic adventure stories.

Dumas went to live in Paris when he was 20 years old. He wrote plays and for magazines, and his plays were so sucessful that he became a full time writer. He then went on to write novels as well.

He used assistants to research some of his books. They came up with plots, often based on historical books, and even wrote large parts of the books, which he then rewrote to add his personal touch. His historical novels, set in earlier periods of French history, were adventurous and exciting. He earned lots of money, but was often poor because he spent the money as quickly as he earned it.

Best known works
The Count of Monte Cristo
The Man in the Iron Mask

Susan Gates

Before Susan became a full-time writer she taught in secondary schools in Africa and England. She has three children and lives in County Durham. Susan has lost count of the number of children's books she has written, but thinks it must be getting close to one hundred.

Susan says, 'I chose *The Three Musketeers* because it's an action-packed, swashbuckling tale full of intrigue, sword fights and frantic, against-the-clock chases. You can almost hear the thundering hooves. The three musketeers Athos, Porthos and Aramis, are all great characters, but I especially like the teenage d'Artagnan, who is stubborn, hot-headed, proud, silly, clumsy, gentle, sharp-witted and amazingly heroic, often all on the same page!'

Notes about this book

This book is set in 17th century France. Many of the adventures that d'Artagnan and his friends get up to are versions of stories that Dumas's mother told him about his father's adventures in the army. However, the idea for the book and the basic plot were not Dumas's. A historian, Maquet, was trying to become a novelist, but he was not a good writer. Together they plotted out the story, and Dumas wrote it in his exciting, colourful style. The book was sold under Dumas's name, and Maquet was paid some money for his contribution. Dumas went on to write two further stories featuring d'Artagnan. *The Three Musketeers* has been made into a musical, a television series and several films.

Page 5
- ***d'Artagnan** The name suggests this man comes from a noble family. In France at this time surnames that began de or d' were names of families who owned land.
- ***musketeers** Soldiers armed with a musket (an old type of rifle). In France, a special unit of musketeers guarded the king and his family.

Page 7
- ***insult** Noble people were proud of their families and they did not want their family name insulted. If a nobleman was insulted he would challenge the person who insulted him to a fight. The fight would 'clear their name', in other words it would keep the family's honour. The fight, either with swords or pistols, did not have to end in death. This kind of fighting was called a duel.

* **lunged** To lunge is to move forward suddenly. It is a common move in sword fighting.
* **cardinal** One of the leading priests in the Roman Catholic Church. The cardinal in France at that time, Cardinal Richelieu, was also an adviser to the king. He was a sly man who wanted to control France. He had many spies and a private army of soldiers who took orders from him and not the king.

Page 10
* **Monsieur** Means 'Mr' in French. Monsieur de Treville was the head of the king's musketeers.

Page 14
* **Lord Buckingham** George Villiers, also called Lord Buckingham, was a real English nobleman who was very important in England in the 17th century.
* **execution** Putting someone to death as a punishment.

Page 21
* **'name the time and the place'** Two people wanting to fight a duel would agree a place and time to do so (usually at dawn or dusk when no one is likely to be around).
* **convent** A building or buildings where nuns live.
* **crowns** Money used at the time.

Page 23
* **duels** A duel is a fight between two people, especially with pistols or swords. Fighting duels in France at this time was illegal, but people still wanted to fight, so they would choose somewhere quiet.

Page 25
* **'act as second'** A second is a person who helps someone fight a duel. A second checked the weapons used, made sure the fight was fair and called for a doctor, if necessary.

Page 26
* **'Better death than dishonour'** A phrase noblemen used because they believed they would rather die than bring dishonour to their family.

Page 29
* **'On guard!'** A phrase that is called out at the beginning of a sword fight. It is a warning to your enemy to put up their sword to protect themselves.
* **to cross swords** To clash swords together – the shape of two swords together looks like an 'X'.
* **cardinal's men** The cardinal had a private army who would do what he told them to do.

Page 30
* **red-handed** To be caught committing a crime.

Page 31
* **veteran** A person with a long history of experience, especially as a soldier.
* **thrust and parried with his rapier** A rapier is a very sharp sword. Thrusting and parrying are sword fighting moves.
* **left-handed** Athos is right-handed, but he is fighting with his left hand to show how skilful he is.

Page 33
* **'Withdraw!'** A command given by the leader of soldiers to run away from a battle they cannot win.

Page 34
* **'All for one and one for all!'** Dumas's motto for the king's musketeers. It suggests that the musketeers will stay loyal and look out for each other.

Page 36
* **flat broke** Means to have no money.

Page 39
* **scour the streets of Paris** Means to look everywhere. This is not as unlikely as it sounds as Paris was quite a small city at the time.
* **Madame** Means 'Mrs' in French.

Page 40
* **gallant** Brave and polite.

Page 47
* **Louvre** A palace in the centre of Paris that is now a famous art gallery and museum.

Page 50
* **tapestry** A piece of strong cloth with pictures or patterns woven or embroidered on it. These were often large and hung from ceiling to floor.
* **lady-in-waiting** A noblewoman who serves or attends to the queen.
* **ruthless politician** Someone involved in governing a country who acts badly and unfairly to make things happen the way they want to.

Page 51
* **eminence** A polite title given to someone famous and respected.

***token** A small gift given to a friend, especially when leaving, to remember them by.

Page 57
***personal seal** At the time, a letter was folded and hot wax was dropped onto the join, to stick the folds together. A ring or 'seal' would then be pressed onto the wax before the wax hardened. The person receiving the letter could tell who had sent it by their seal and know if the letter had already been opened.
***doublet** A man's jacket worn in the 17th century.

Page 61
***his blood was up** Means he was very angry.

Page 62
***ambush** A sudden, surprise attack from a hidden place.

Page 64
***traitors** A traitor is someone who betrays their country or friends.

Page 66
***tide turned** You could only take a ship out from the port of Calais when the tide was high. If the tide went down, you would have to wait 12 hours before the tide rose again and you could take a ship to England.
***ran him through** To harm someone by sticking a sword into them.

Page 69
***captors** People who catch a person and keep them prisoner.